G000153383

Contents

are the single biggest influence
on how motivated **your team** feel,

not the company

not senior managers

but YOU. Use this power to good effect,

more to achieve more.

To:

From:

WORK ON FULL POWER

To get the best from others,
inspire the best you can.

The equation is clear.

Give more and you get more back.

You'll find your power **increases** when you make your team feel high powered.

So boost inner strength and you'll unleash the power people have but rarely use.

Do you achieve results and	**E**ncourage people along the way?
Do you challenge your team to go one better and	**N**ote the small things individuals do that make the big difference?
Do you demand high standards and	**E**nthuse others every step of the way?
Do you stay focused on the big things and	**R**ecognise the effort people put in?
Do you expect more and	**G**ive more - consistently?
Do you deliver the numbers	**Y**et still make time for your team?

There's a big difference between working on half power and **full power.**

On the left it's all about task and on the right it's about people. When you do right by your people, you unleash **ENERGY.** This positive force helps people to win.

There's a world of difference
between being . . .

A   NUMBER

and feeling

Inspired people work 'full-on'
and as a result achieve **MORE**.

This little book is all about the
small things that make the

DIFFERENCE

How do you ensure people don't just turn up -
but are turned on to win?

Can you get the job done **AND** inspire people?

Do you think creatively and inspire your people
during the good times and tough times?

It's clear. You win when you create

It's called working on **'full power'**.

When team members feel powerful – they walk **tall**.

When they feel **INSPIRED** –
they take pride in their work.

When they feel energised – they take on the **UGLY**
aspects of the job and do it well.

This is called 'flow' state, where people are so
absorbed in doing a good job they

Act, **T**hink and **B**ehave – as though they work for
themselves first and the company second. It's that
magical moment, where people expect more from
themselves than their manager. They dare to aim high.

Chances are your high performers take

ACCOUN**T**A**B**ILITY.

As a manager this is what counts.
It's the true mark of your ability.

INSPIRED people seem to have more stamina, resilience, tenacity, pride, passion and enthusiasm. They have an abundance of energy to make things happen and get things done.

Your job is to keep the energy . . . **flowing**

Save energy.
Remove the road blocks that **STOP** your team. It's liberating when individuals don't have to work with one-hand tied behind their back. Trust your people - limit the rules. **Cut the** bureaucracy. ✂

Have fun and promote the flow of **creative energy.**

Spark the imagination, it fires people up to . . .

Provide encouragement and generate positive energy. With self belief team members back themselves to succeed.

They have a **GO**.

Boost energy. Connect people to their goals. Challenge and support your team in equal measure. Never be satisfied with second best. Develop winners. Get the best from each player in your team.

Energised people work with purpose. They're switched on to their goals, plugged in to the company's values and turned on by fulfilling their potential.

Nothing remarkable gets done . . .

. . . when your team feels small.

When **YOU** put TASK before people,

motivating people becomes an uphill

TASK

And whenever your people are a ^Second thought, don't be surprised if you get second best.

It's simple.

Without energy there is no power.

Without power there is no *drive.*

Without *drive*, people don't push
themselves to do more.

Be the energy source.

Inspire people to succeed.

High performance depends on it.

Start **NOW**. Don't put it off.
Get into the habit of inspiring your team.
Use positive power over status power.

Make a fuss over people when they do the **small things** well. And, you'll find they do the big stuff, with the minimum of fuss.

Inspired people are attentive even when the work is mundane.

They find ways to make an unglamorous job glamorous. They think more creatively, persevere more, show more courage – and why?

They expect more from *themselves* than anyone else.

This is the power of inspiration.

> "THE FIGHT IS WON OR LOST FAR AWAY FROM WITNESSES – BEHIND THE LINES, IN THE GYM AND OUT THERE ON THE ROAD, LONG BEFORE I DANCE UNDER THOSE LIGHTS"

MUHAMMED ALI

Success looks effortless, only when people have put the effort in.

Work with your team and define personalised goals - that have **full colour**, surround sound and set the heart racing.

People put the effort in, when they have absolute clarity on what they're striving for. They stick with it, through **thick** and thin, even when there is no one there watching over them.

The only place where

'SUCCESS'

comes before

'WORK'

is in the dictionary.

Vidal Sassoon

Let's not kid ourselves. It takes **hard work** and **determination** to succeed. And as a manager you have a vital role to play. You can either boss people about or **inspire** them to work hard. It's your call.

HOW POWERFUL DO YOU MAKE YOUR PEOPLE FEEL?

Circle the rating your team would give **you** on the 'power chart' . . .

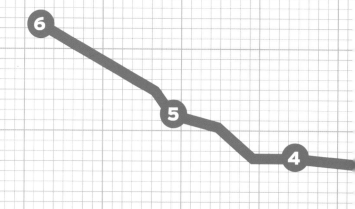

6 Inspires us to jump tall buildings

5 Motivates us to jump townhouses

4 Encourages us to jump and do the best we can

3 Tells us to "jump when I say jump"

2 "You jump and I'll watch"

1 "No jumping. You'll probably get hurt"

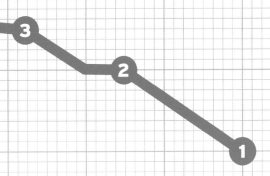

You can't force high performance – but you can be a positive force.

Connect people to their goals. When team members emotionally connect with their goals they start believing in what they're doing.

Energise team members by maintaining positive working relationships. People thrive in trust based relationships.

Support people to **SHINE** by developing their skills and know-how. By unleashing potential you power performance.

Switch people on by boosting confidence. People live up or live down to the expectations you have of them. Play to people's strengths and back them to succeed.

HARDWIRE THE RIGHT BEHAVIOURS AND HIGH PERFORMANCE WILL FOLLOW.

When your team don't feel powerful, you soon see it. They keep a low profile, fail to use their judgement and pass the buck. Work becomes a chore and energy is wasted on the wrong things.

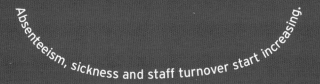

Absenteeism, sickness and staff turnover start increasing.

So make no mistake. When you focus on the task at the expense of your team – there are real costs. Both to the business and to your reputation. To add insult to injury, you end up short-changing your team.

There is no doubt, getting the is important.

But it's only half-done. People come into work for more than just picking up a salary cheque. If this is all you demand from people, this is all they will give you.

Half-hearted, half done and half-measured is wholly unacceptable.

You have to sustain the human spirit.
It is a power source and from it springs

passion,
pride
and
purpose.

The big prize is getting the job done willingly and well, with highly motivated people. So create the **buzz** and inspire electrifying performance.

It's simple to say but **tough** to do.

It's all too easy to slip into your comfort-zone. Head-down, chasing deadlines and sticking to how you've always done things.

comfort-zone

At times like this, creatively leading your people - - - - - flies out the window.

Challenge yourself to lead.

POWERFUL LESSONS

Learn to lead.

When you become a manager of others,
it's not about you.

Learn to play down yourself and build up others.
When it's **your** ideas, **your** decisions, **your** views,
your goals, **your** challenges -

it's one big yawn. zzzzzzzzzzz

People switch off.

When people switch off, you end up doing more.

In striving to be a leading light,
it's too easy to burn out.

It's not good for you and it's certainly not good
for the team. If it gets to that stage, where you
want to throw in the towel, pick it up and mop
your brow.

P a c e   y o u r s e l f
and learn to *fast-track* team performance.

When it's all about you - be warned.

In the end you'll become resentful.
The team will resent your leadership style
and your partner will resent the fact you
are never there.

When managers become resentful,
they make poor decisions.

Anger and frustration don't sit well with

Can you give **3 good reasons**
why anyone should be led by you?

When you're not clear what you
stand for, you'll f ll for anything.

a

It's not enough to just show up.

Show the **real** you.
The **real** person not the mask.

When your team know what you **care** about –
they engage.

When they see your **passion** –
it rubs off on them.

When they understand your **aspirations** –
they rally together.

Strong leadership and **strong performance**
go hand-in-hand.

Be a great coach and see it as real work.
The more you do it, the better you'll be.

Respect team members by genuinely listening.
Show empathy by putting yourself in their shoes.
Encourage others to talk without fear.

When you get this level of honesty, performance
conversations get to a new level.

They're real, relevant and rewarding.
This is the power of honesty.

When you level with people, you help them to
reach the next level of performance.

Put more into your Trust Account
than you draw out.

Trust Account ⏻

Be consistent
Be honest
Be there for your team

2834 3215 7980 6678

Be consistent.

Be honest.

Be there for your team.

Be true to you.

It's too easy to become a suit –
following company policies and procedures.

Live your values.

Learn to have humility.

Lead the heart and manage the head.

Let go of ------

Learn to take pride in others' success.

Credit others' ideas in your work. And let team members attend high profile meetings.

It takes a big person to put their team first.

Admit to your ~~mist~~ mistakes.

When you're big enough to do that,
so will others.

Get things in the open.

~~Take the learning~~

Take the learning from mistakes
and FREE PEOPLE TO ACT.

It's easy to try too hard to be the perfect manager. In trying to look good, you miss the good ideas of others.

In trying to be in control of everything, the world starts revolving around you.

Approvals land on your desk.

Decisions land on your head.

Customer problems land in your lap.

So is it any wonder some managers rarely take a holiday, or dare take a day out of their business.

They see it as their neck on the line.
But there is a better way.

Learn to develop the people around **you**

Learn to
grow
grow
grow
grow
grow
grow with your role.

This will mean unlearning old habits as well as learning new behaviours.

Role model the behaviours you expect from others. If you want others to raise their game - you have to role model this.

If you want team members to have meaningful personal development plans, you will be living yours with a **passion.**

The powerful lesson?

When YOU learn to grow, you grow to lead.

Leadership and 'followership' are two sides of the same coin. So why should anyone follow you?

PULLING POWER

Do you inspire people to think for themselves or instruct people to follow your orders?

STOP being so busy.

START being more productive.

STOP having all the answers.

START asking the right questions.

STOP talking quite so much.

START listening.

STOP never being there for your team.

START being present.

STOP trying to be the hero.

START creating heroes.

STOP being a star.

START building a star team.

'Push' style influencing is needed in business – but use it s p a r i n g l y . It relies on you instructing, telling, directing and pushing for action.

It's like pushing water up hill. It's hard work – both for you and the team. It works best when you're fire fighting. So be selective in its use.

'Pull' style influencing is about building for the future. You encourage greater ownership, participation and enthusiasm from your team.

You delegate more, trust more and give more responsibility. It can seem scary, but when you 'pull it off', the prize is worth it – a high performing team.

You insp1re high performance by making people feel powerful. Here are 10 practical ways you can boost inner strength.

1 You **in**spire by boosting my self confidence

2 You **in**spire by playing to my strengths

3 You **in**spire by seeking my ideas and keeping me in the picture

4 You **in**spire by showing an interest in me and my work

5 You **in**spire by noticing the small things I do that make a big difference

6 You **in**spire by giving me the benefit of the doubt

7 You **in**spire by saying 'thank you' for a job well done

8 You **in**spire by being honest with me

9 You **in**spire by setting aside quality time for me

10 You **in**spire by trusting me

When your team members have **inner strength – they 'punch above their weight'.** They don't fret about their position on the organisational chart.

Seek to **in**spire by building **in**ner strength and you'll find people take a real interest in their work.

How people feel on the inside...

...influences...

...their performance.

When people feel **powerful** -
they give their discretionary goodwill.

They start caring about their work,
when they see you care.

But it does not happen over night.
You and your team have to work at it.

So have no doubt. It takes **TIME.**
You have to invest time.

There is a timeless truth.
You reap what you sow.

You will find 101 excuses why you can't find enough time. But you DO have a choice. You have to be ruthless about what you say 'yes' to and what you say 'no' to.

"I've got too much work on..."

"Can we do it another time please?..."

"I got stuck in traffic . . ."

"Some other time..."

"My schedule is full . . ."

"I'll do it in a bit...
just not now"

"I've got a meeting so i won't have time..."

"IT WAS LATE
SO I DIDN'T
GET A
CHANCE . "

"Can't be bothered right now . . ."

"I'll do it in a bit... just not now"

"there are more important things"

48

You'll never see an individual's hidden depths . . .

. . . if email email email email email ema
email email email email email email ema
email you're email email email email ema
email email email email email email ema
email email sinking email email email ema
email email email email email email ema
email email email email email email ema
email email email up to email email ema
email email email email email email ema
email email email email email email ema
email email email email email email ema
email email email email email your ema
email email email email email email ema
email email email email email email ema
email email email email email email ema
email email email email email email ema
email email email email email email ema
email email email email email email ema
email email email email email email ema
email email email email email email ema
email email email email email email ema
email email email email email email ema
email email email email email email ema

49

nail	email	email	email	email	email	email
nail	email	email	email	email	email	email
nail	email	email	email	email	email	email
nail	email	email	email	email	email	email
nail	email	email	email	email	email	email
nail	email	email	email	email	email	email
nail	email	email	email	email	email	email
nail	email	email	email	email	email	email
nail	email	email	email	email	email	email
nail	email	email	email	email	email	email
nail	email	email	email	email	email	email
nail	email	email	email	email	email	email
nail	email	email	email	email	email	email
nail	email	neck	email	email	email	email
nail	email	email	email	email	email	email
nail	email	email	email	in	email	email
nail	email	email	email	email	email	email
nail	email	email	email	email	email	email
nail	email	email	email	email	email	email
nail	email	email	email	email	email	email
nail	email	email	email	email	email	email
nail	email	email	email	email	email	email
nail	email	email	email	email	email	emails

It's hard to enthuse

and energise others,

when you're running

on

empty.

Remember . . .
It's tough to win titles when you pull rank
and use your job title to get things done.

And . . .
You win in business when you make it
your business to inspire your team to be
the best they can.

Be a talent spotter.

Work with each team member to be the best they can. What are they good at? What do they have a flair for? What do they loathe doing?

Nothing 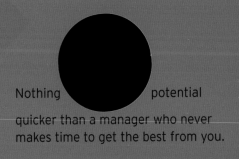 potential quicker than a manager who never makes time to get the best from you.

Inspire people by spotting skills and talent they may not see in themselves.

No doubt they'll have rough edges.
But have patience. Experience is a great teacher.

And to mature, people have to make their own mistakes. Just be on hand to pick people up and help dust them down after a fall.

To spot   you have to be on
the spot.   Take a real interest in
how people   perform. And if you
manage remotely - seek feedback from people
on the spot.

You will always be faced with pressing priorities.
But you just have to press ahead
and prioritise **one-to-one time . . .**

and recognise the s ki ls people have.

Twenty minutes of 'light bulb' conversations
per individual, per week. Are people using their
skills to best effect?

Use this time for **re-focusing**, **re-invigorating**
and **re-charging** the batteries.

Inspiring others is not a soft option.

We have already established you have
to be **ruthless** with your time.

Be **tough** on under-performance.

Be **disciplined** by focusing on the 'important'
and not just the 'urgent'.

Have the **courage** to trust in others.

Be **brave** in never settling for second best.

Let's dispel one myth. Inspiring others is NOT
about being nice. It's about providing high support
and high challenge. It's about expecting more by
giving more.

When your peers appear busy sitting in front of their lap tops or on the phone to customers, or in wall-to-wall meetings - it may seem you're swimming against the tide. You may question why you're spending twenty minutes per week, per colleague in supporting their performance.

One-to-ones,

coaching,

feedback,

celebrating success - is real work.

You have to dare to be different.

Lead, don't follow the crowd.

crowd
crowd
crowd crowd
crowd crowd
crowd crowd crowd
crowd crowd
crowd crowd
crowd crowd
crowd crowd
crowd crowd
crowd crowd
crowd
crowd

"IF YOU ACCEPT THE EXPECTATIONS OF OTHERS, ESPECIALLY NEGATIVE ONES, THEN YOU NEVER WILL CHANGE THE OUTCOME."

MICHAEL JORDON.

Be your own person. Avoid group think.

Set a **POSITIVE** agenda. Create winners.

No excuses.

P⏻WER FAILURE

Ten of the worst excuses you hear as to why managers fail to inspire.

I don't have enough time.

This applies to 99.9% of managers.

If it's important you'll make time.
100 minutes per month per team member is
what you should be aiming for - 20 minutes
a week. Is that asking too much?

Ask more from yourself before you ask
more from others.

> # This company only judges me on the results I get.

This is a common mistake managers make.
Most companies who are results oriented, know their most expensive resource is people. They expect a good manager to deliver the numbers through their team. Make no mistake. If you're hitting the numbers but seen as a poor manager to work for, it will be on someone's radar screen.

If you're not hitting the numbers and have a reputation for being a poor people manager – the clock is ticking.

I don't get inspired by my manager.

You don't have to be – so long as you inspire your team. When you practice what you preach, you can start demanding more from your manager.

> **I am out with customers, doing 'real' work and don't see enough of my team**

Well done on adding value to your customers. Now find a way to service your customers **and** your team. You have to do both. It comes with the job and is non-negotiable. If all you want to do is service customers, maybe you should consider not being a manager.

Be creative and find a way to get enthused by managing your team. What happens 'in here' determines what happens 'out there' with your clients. The stronger your team, the mo>e value you o££er your clients.

> We work in a *fast paced* business: I can't plan my one-to-ones.
> The goal-posts keep changing and I can't really review performance.

If you focus on the person rather than the task, you'll have loads to discuss. Allow team members to lead your informal one-to-ones.
The one thing that pleases them about their **personal effectiveness** and the one thing they can improve for the week ahead.

Show an interest in your team and they'll show an interest in their work. The research evidence for this simple truth is well documented.

> **My job is not to win popularity contests. It's to deliver results.**

Delivering results is good.

Delivering results through highly motivated people is even better.

You don't have to be popular to inspire others. Expect more by giving more. Start with sharing feedback. Praise high performance and provide recognition. This simple act is rocket fuel. It boosts confidence. And with regular coaching, connects people to their goals. If you do this consistently, you'll get consistently high results.

It's not rocket science.

When you're disciplined with your time and you coach you are less likely to discipline for under-performance.

> **If people want to be inspired they're in the wrong job or with the wrong company.**
> **I'm not a magician and business is tough.**

When business is tough, that's precisely the time to inspire others. By getting the extra 10% from each and every team member, you make a big difference to overall performance. It's tough to inspire others in difficult times, but not impossible - it's called leadership!

Inspiring stronger performance beats finding performance improvement through cost cutting, efficiency savings, lay-offs and re-structuring.

To raise the bar, you need to raise morale.

I don't have the mon£y or the resources to inspire people.

Inspiring others is rarely about money. It's about the free things - like positive working relationships, having a manager who shows an interest in you and your work. It's this sense of belonging, feeling valued and needed that inspires people.

Grand gestures don't work. **Sincerity rules.**

I'm not the 'rarr-rarr' type.

You're just the type then. 'Rarr-rarr' works when it's done in moderation - say once a year.

That leaves you 11 months to patiently inspire others. Make the time for your team, listen to how you can get the best from each individual and act on it.

Reflective types can inspire too, so long as they remember to build trust based relationships.

I'm a trained professional first and a manager second.

This one wears thin quickly.

It speaks volumes about you – "I love the technical aspects of my role and find the people side a chore".

Simply put, your team deserves better.
The one non-negotiable when you're a leader,
is you need 'followers'.

Customers and clients benefit when your team is high performing. Potential problems get nipped in the bud, by those who are closest to the customer.

Things don't get escalated to you –
giving you the head room to innovate.

Reflect on this. The strength of your team reflects on you.

Team power always delivers better results than the power of one person.

P⏻WERLESS

Here are the most common ways a manager can make team members feel small and diminish their power.

You diminish power when . . .

You insist people do things your way
and this is the only way.

By not being open to others' ideas,
you close down your team's creativity.

You shut-off the oxygen that keeps things fresh.
No one person has a monopoly on good ideas.
And stale ideas lead to tired performanczzzzzz

You diminish power when . . .

People falter when you only find fault. It is human nature. When we fear falling, we take small, tentative steps. Self protection becomes more important than pushing yourself and performance suffers.

You diminish power when . . .

You belittle people with, **sarcasm,**
INAPPROPRIATE HUMOUR
and unguarded comments.

The result is predictable. Your team become
guarded. With defences up they will be slow to
trust you.

People watch their backs, when you **rubbish**
others behind their backs.

You diminish power when . . .

You have favourites, treat people inc^{o}ns$_i$ste^{n}tl$_y$ and regularly lose your TEMPER.

Uncertainty creates anxiety – never a good climate for high performance. You put doubt in people's minds.

Their thinking goes something like this:
"if you can't manage your emotions, what can you manage?"

You diminish power when . . .

You take the limelight and the credit
for your team's efforts.

You force people to stay in your shadow.

They find other places where they can shine -
outside hobbies, interests and social activities.

**Worst case scenario, your better people join
your competitors.**

You diminish power when . . .

You look after **No.1**, taking all the

Glamour work yourself.

When you win and your team lose – you lose big time. It's an own goal and self-inflicted. It shows no sensitivity to the needs of others.

Such selfishness breeds contempt. And as a result, quality, morale, team work, customer service – all fade.

You diminish power when . . .

You only let people know how they are performing, when things go w r o n g

This simply focuses your team's mind on minimising mistakes -
not maximising opportunities.

You form subjective judgements of team members, label them and treat them accordingly.

People live up or live down to your expectations.

What do you see?

Write down your judgements:

_____

_____

_____

_____

_____

_____

See page 84 for the answer.

When we form judgements - we see what we want to see and hear what we want to hear. We end up being selective.

Never stop believing, people have it within themselves to be 1% more effective than last month.

Now ACT on it.

People **fly** and take their performance to new heights, when they have optimism, self belief and self conviction. An unshakeable belief they will succeed at whatever they put their mind to.

It's called
HOPE and it's what strong leaders provide.

POWER SURGE

Ten ways to boost performance: get more by giving more.

You may not find one-to-one time with team members inspiring. But it's not about **you**. It's about the **team.** By showing a genuine interest in people and their work, you significantly increase the odds of successful delivery.

1. You don't have to like people to inspire them.

   Be fair,

   Be consistent,

   Be objective.

   Focus on behaviours not personality.

   Catch people doing things well.

2. Play to **STRENGTHS.** Find ways to redesign the role around the individual.

Respect the individual and make every effort to help them succeed. If they're part of your team, you owe it to them.

3. Role model the way.

You have to **earn respect** first.

When you lead without title, you encourage others to take leadership.

4. Fix the '**show stoppers**'.

It's hard to inspire when basic things are not right. Find the 5 most common 'show stoppers' and work with the team to fix them.

Do your people have the right information, the right tools and the right skills to succeed?

5. Challenge the fear of failure.

Encourage people to use their judgement to power through problems.

Encourage decisions to be made locally. Provide a few boundaries, but then free people to act.

6. Check in with people and check out what's frustrating them. Away from the desk and over a coffee, create a safe place to listen. Then check back and agree what actions each of you will take.

Have regular performance health checks, as prevention is better than cure.

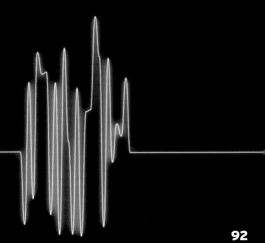

7. Build self esteem.

Individuals censor themselves, when they lack self confidence.

They believe they'll fail before they've even taken action. They wait for someone else to take the lead. Or they wait for APPROVAL

While they wait, others have to carry the **weight.**

8. Challenge the unacceptable.

Use your passion to fire up others.

You need people who are ready to voice their ideas. So count your blessings every time a team member voices an opinion. Don't pay lip service, find ways to make it work. It might take two or three fine tunings – but then, let them run with it.

When people put their name to their work, they're underwriting it. They personally see to it.

9. Keep your own little book.

The **HIGHS** and **LOWS** of each team member's performance.

When people know you take an interest in their work - they self manage their performance.

Write rich examples in your little book, to enrich your coaching. **Reward the right behaviour.**

Make it your cause to **INSPIRE** and others will perspire for the cause.

10. Ensure the rate of learning is greater than the rate of change.
RL>RC.

When your team have personal mastery and feel on top of their game, they start behaving like top performers. Call it inner confidence. But it inspires people to take calculated risks.

It's mind over matter.

Self belief triumphs over self doubt.

You no longer have victims of change –
but a team who seize the moment.
Shaping their future before someone else does.

POWER SHIFT

Can you make the shift
from being a star to
developing a star team?

It's not what's in front of you that blocks the way, it's what's inside that holds you back.

Anon

Learn to love your role as a leader.

Make the *shift*

When your team live with . . .

. . . **poor communication,** they learn to survive on rumours

. . . **instructions,** they learn to stop thinking for themselves in work

. . . **targets,** they learn to compete with each other

. . . **deadlines,** they learn to fire fight

. . . **problems,** they learn to be pessimistic

. . . **cynicism,** they learn to be bitter

. . . **unrealistic goals,** they learn to disengage

. . . **criticism,** they learn to self-doubt

What a difference YOU can make.

It's too easy to fill your diary with the urgent, tangible, real life problems. The ones that give you job satisfaction when you sort them out. Job done and you can tick it off your to-do list.

Managing people is rarely so straightforward. It's not always easy to measure the impact of your coaching. So don't revert back to type.

Make the *shift*.

From putting out fires, to putting a fire in the belly.

As a professional, intellect counts.

As a manager, emotional intelligence rates highly.

Learn to know your team and the unique qualities each individual brings to it. Each individual has their own signature strengths.

Celebrate them.

Build on them.

Maximise them.

Make the *shift*.

Use IQ and EQ in equal measure.

Re-invent yourself when you progress to a manager.
You are **more** than your job title.

Make the *shift.*

From an Accountant to a ...	Manager who sees the ROI in people
From a Surveyor to a ...	Manager who builds talent
From a Lawyer to a ...	Manager who looks for fact-based evidence in raising performance
From a Doctor to a ...	Manager who builds a healthy business
From a Trader to a ...	Manager who invests in developing the potential in people
From a Banker to a ...	Manager who returns profit through people

Build your

Personal Brand

by supporting the career development of team members.

When your reputation as a strong coach proceeds you - you'll be in demand.
You will attract the best people to your team. And be in demand as a mentor.

Make the *shift.*

Focus on building the talent in your team,
by building your own talent as a coach.
It's a highly marketable skill.

Your business will be more successful if you get an extra 10% performance from your high performers than an extra 10% from your under performers.

Yet some managers invest more time with the latter than the former. If your time is a precious resource, you're rewarding the wrong behaviour.

Make the *shift*.

Spend more time with your high performers. Recognise them, retain them and reward them with high profile assignments. High performers need inspiring too.

You get what you tolerate. Set your standards and expectations. Reinforce what is OK performance and what isn't. Morale and motivation suffer when you start making allowances for under-performance.

Make the *shift.*

Don't compensate for under-performance, address it.

Don't tolerate under-performance, challenge it.

Don't rubbish the person. Reinforce the right behaviours and redress the inappropriate ones.

Recruit people who have headroom to grow.

↑   ↑

You can be sure your business will change 12-18 months from now. New roles and role profiles will emerge from a new organisational structure. People with headroom use their head and see the opportunities change presents.

So make the *shift.*

Recruit for attitude and train for skill.

Recruit for the current role and the next move.

Recruit people who are clearly better than the people you have. It should never be about putting bums on seats.

Inspire your team by bringing the best people 'out there', 'in here'.

Have a 'stop-doing' list.

Make the *shift.*

Being busy is not the same as being productive.

Be selective about what you say **'yes'** to –
everything can't be a priority.

Create thinking time – shape your future,
or someone else will.

Learn to manage your boss –

its too easy to over-commit, to over-promise

and under-deliver.

Get close to your front line colleagues. They're often closer to your customer than you. You need strong leadership here too.

Make the *shift.*

From being in meetings to being accessible.

From being a name on an organisational chart to being a face people connect with.

From talking corporate speak to listening and acting on the ideas front line colleagues have for improving service.

From being a BIG CHEESE to being a CHEERLEADER.

Make time for

When people are free to laugh,
you know they're happy to be there.

Make the *shift.*

Work hard and play hard.

From being serious, to getting serious about
building positive working relationships.

Focus on business KPIs and the human KPIs
(Keep People Inspired).

You have the power to inspire high performance.
Focus on four key drivers:

Gain commitment to goals,

Energise working relationships,

Take competence to a new level,

Build confidence to win.

Light up performance
with Willing and Able Talented Teams.

Lighting up

How do you get results? Tick the statement that applies to you most of the time.

- [ ] I get results through inspiring people: I always build self belief and commit to helping individuals fulfil their potential.

- [ ] I get results through coaching: I always support individuals to play to their strengths and to set higher expectations of themselves.

- [ ] I get results through feedback: I always let each individual know what they're doing well and what improvements they need to make.

- [ ] I get results through motivation: I always praise the positives and encourage people to do their best.

- [ ] I get results through delegation: I always share priorities and responsibilities to the right people.

Performance

☐ I get results through clear goal setting:
so each team member always knows what
is expected of them.

☐ I get results through drive: if I can see things
aren't getting done, I do it myself.

☐ I get results through micro-managing:
I check things are done to my standards.

☐ I get results through survival of the fittest:
the good ones stay and the poor ones leave.

☐ I get results through fear: get this done or
your job's on the line.

What do you need to . . .

Stop doing?

Start doing?

Continue doing?

Go to our website:
www.100wattcoaching.com
for great ideas on how to use this book
for conferences and teambuilding:

10 inspiring activities
for your conference

10 powerful teambuilding
activities for your away-days.

W.A.T.T POWER

Achieving high performance with
Willing and Able Talented Teams

High performance starts and ends with one simple truth. Learn how to get the best from people -

one

individual

at

a

time.

It's not about getting the best people or even being the best. It's about inspiring people to be the best they can, month in, month out. Who are willing and able to give to the cause.

WILLING

Commitment is achieved when people are connected to their goals.	Energy Switching people on through supportive working relationships.

- + +

ABLE

- **Competence**
Mastering the skills to be a leading light. **+** **Confidence**
A positive mindset to take on challenging work and succeed. **+**

100 WATT Coaching - Lighting Up Performance™.
A high performance toolkit and 12 month methodology.

At Tools For Leading Change Ltd (TLC) we are a team of Organisational Development Consultants. Our expertise lies in creating high performance, by hardwiring the right behaviours.

How are we different?

- We keep our workshops real and focus on live business challenges.

- We don't use power-point or course manuals. We use a Coaching Toolkit.

- We are Business Psychologists and focus on raising self awareness.

- We allow line managers to track team motivation with our on-line questionnaire.

- We use professional actors for developing coaching skills and sharing feedback.

- We help raise performance by developing line managers from 'green belt', to 'purple belt' to 'black belt' in coaching.

- Participants use a Talent Development Tool. They develop a game plan for raising the performance of each individual in their team.

- We know high performance is about doing things differently and we invite participants to invest 100 minutes per month coaching each team member.

Our leading workshop is:

- 100 WATT Coaching - Lighting Up Performance™.
  To find out more, go on our website:
  www.100wattcoaching.com

- To pilot our workshops within your business,
  select 12 participants for a two day workshop with
  a one day follow up workshop, after 100 days.
  We will adapt the content to ensure it hits the
  mark for your business. We also train the trainer
  to ensure high performance behaviours are
  hardwired into your business.

Finally, please share your feedback on this handbook
with me: **sukhwant@toolsforleadingchange.com**
or call on **0845 607 6878**

*The word 'inspire' appears five times on the cover.

There are always more ways than you think to inspire
people at work. You just have to look for them.

In your 'p⏻wer pack' you'll find 28 statements.

Step 1 Sort each statement under 3 clusters.
        Is it 'critical', 'important' or 'desirable'
        for inspiring your team right now?

Step 2 Take the items in each cluster and sort them
        into their headings: commitment, energy,
        competence, confidence.

Step 3 Under 'critical' which headings have
        the most cards?

Step 4 Under 'important' which headings have
        the most cards?

Step 5 Under 'desirable' which headings have
        the most cards?

Step 6 What does this tell you about what your team
        needs from you right now?

Step 7 Over the next quarter what actions will
        you take?

NOTES

Sukhwant leads a team of Corporate Psychologist and OD Consultants at TLC (Tools For Leading Change Ltd). Our aim is to inspire high performance using 'power tools'. We have spent 10 years developing a complete methodology for creating high performance and have been privileged to work with fantastic clients. In the past few years over 2,000 managers have experienced '100 WATT Coaching – Lighting Up Performance™'. This book gives you a snapshot into our work.

We provide:

- Managers with practical coaching tools, so they provide high support and high challenge coaching. We call it 'light bulb conversations'.

- Individuals with the tools to manage their own motivation, so they engage in striving to be their personal best.

- HR Business Partners with quarterly motivation data, so they can influence key decision makers